CW01502103

ACKNOWLEDGMENTS

I would like to say thank you to all the people ho have helped in the creation of this collection, from the friends and family who pushed and encouraged me to publish the poems, to the people who will never know that their place in even just a fleeting moment of my life have made some of these poems possible.
Please enjoy.

1. CHILDHOOD

The Nativity (Class 1b)

Michael and Esther, you're Joseph and Mary
Michael stop crying, Jesus is not scary
Brian, Wendy and David - you'll do for the Wise Men,
(Don't give Brian the crowns, you know he'll just lick them)
We still need the angel, better Kerry than Lorraine,
After all we can't have the angel screaming obscenities at Elaine,
who has been made the Head Shepherd, over Fraser and Paul
And now that row about "the Barbie" isn't ending at all.
So Lorraine sit with Mandy, no, she won't pick her nose.
Just stop your whining and you can be sheep I suppose.
That still leaves the cow, raise your hands in the air...
Just hands please Christine, we don't want to see underwear,
Louise and Sam, do you think you can be the donkey?
Sam you're the back end, and it's a donkey, not a "monkey".
Duncan, oh dear, ummm can you be a horse, and go "clip clop"?
No Louise the horse and donkey won't need to "go plop".
So I think that is everything, who doesn't have a part?
Oh dear Fiona, stop sobbing and we'll make you "the star".
Now settle down children, it'll be magical (with luck),
And nobody's part is "the bestest", so if your unhappy you can get to...
the headteacher's office!

Nightmares

Tiny key
Small door
Don't go in
You won't get out

School Yard

I see you,
Cowering,
Behind a small group of gathered boys.
Through the flurry
Of fists and feet

I see you.

I try to fade away
Into the concrete,
Where gravel and sand bite into my face,
And it's the dust in my eyes
That makes me cry.

You see me

And do nothing.
Even in numbers
You stand in fear that you might be next
To face the fear.
Lose your pride.

I lose it.

Pride, fear, pain,
Nothing left,
but to fight back and become what we hate
And allow that rage
To destroy
Our identity.

All victims

The bell.
End of round.
Crowds disperse and head for classes
And left alone
Torn and bruised
Cut and lost

Aware always
That you
And

I did nothing

A Child's Wish

The red nylon trousers crackle and pop
As I slide up on your knee
Your beard is cottonwool and string
And you hide underneath

I see your hair is brown, not white
And you smell like fags and cheese
And my mum tells me to be polite
And remember to say, "please".

Your helper has her pointy ears
Which are two different sizes
Plastic reindeer can't do very much
And this music mum despises

The last girl cried an awful lot
She asked you for a kitten
You just shoved a doll at her
With yellow "Claus" in fingerless mittens

This grotto is not real I'm sure
It's scented with other kid's wee
And by the looks of the junk you're handing out
I can tell why the presents are free

I don't think you are really him
And you look too drunk to care
But since mum swears you really are him
What I wish for is a teddy bear...

'Time For Bed,' Said Zebedee

Heavy eyes
Weighed down by hours without rest
Are fought at every turn
In their attempt to
Stop me
From keeping on
Keeping on.

Cotton wads,
Phantom and invisible,
Pack my mouth
And dry my resolve
And prevent me
From crying 'help'

I drown in quick sands
Of time
As further
And further
I fall away
From any sense of reality
Until the clarity of waking life
Is too blurred to be real
And my world descends
Into the darkness
Behind closed lids.

Santa's Gift

With shaking hands and thumping heart
I tip toe down the stairs
I want to catch Old St. Nick
Completely unawares.

But it's too late he's been and gone
And there beneath the tree
Are lots of shiny sparkly treats
Boxed and wrapped for me.

I stand stock still with open mouth
And my eyes are filled with tears
The tree is lit like the midnight sky
And music fills my ears.

The sound of voices singing low
So sweet with joy and love
And my eyes are drawn towards the sky
To the sight of cherubim above.

And all at once I'm no longer home
The world it swirls and shifts
And windows onto wet town streets
Are filled with crisp snowdrifts

A figure, large and draped in red
Sits smiling by the hearth
A hearty laugh gusts past his lips
And soothes my quickening heart.

Upon his knee I take my place
And such warmth I feel inside
For Father Christmas has this night
Chosen not to hide.

All too soon I wake again
And in my room with no sight of those toys
But still I feel the warmth and love
And wonderment and peace and joy.

The Art of War

Armistice was sounded
That sixteenth day, in that cold, cold November.
Windowpanes rattled
In the winter winds;
A drum roll to mark the silence of truce
The innocent and injured marked the moment
And raised their heads and hearts
From below abused, tagged and gum stained desks
Hand raised
An order for calm
And young Jamie sheltered the final victim
With an arm of desperate comfort
Eyes well
As she grasps
Her face
The developing, stinging, red welt
A signal to all
That a cease-fire

Was the only final solution
Crumpled and limp
Long dead projectiles
And missiles
Litter the wooden rows of trenches,
Which stand proud
In the last rays of the dying afternoon sun,
And hang from wall posters
And hang from light fittings
And hang from chalkboards
Sanity returned
To the classroom
Differences forgotten
The heat of battle subsides
Leaving only scarring memory
At the end of the last, great
Elastic Band War

I Had a Strange Dream

Pandas
Bathed in moonlight
Bathe in my bath
Wrapped in cotton towel
Cotton wool wrapped
Protecting
Pandas.

Cycling pandas
Bicycle
By cycle
Round the town
All around
Until they fall
Dizzy
And dazed.

Sleeping pandas
Sleep heavy
Heavy pandas
In bed
Dreaming
Of me.

A Last Goodbye

In the vestiges of my mind,
I will not lose the memories of childhood times,
Life's circle cannot rob
Things and places that will return.
Ashes to ashes,
As beginning to end to beginning.
I will not lock away childish things,
I will not fear the end as time's bell tolls.
The light of youth still burns from the fire,
And glowing embers of laughter crackle in the grate.

The cold mists of times much older,
Cloud my eyes with tears of joy
And the pain of losing friends and places
Turn my head away
From the places I have gone before
I remember
A house which rang with sounds of games,
A broken toy which was put away
I remember,
Nothing that makes my time any easier
Except perhaps the fear of having known them.
And having known
Knowing nothing

Nothing lasts forever
But in the end
Everything starts again.

Childhood Summer

Run, run away
Run, run.

Through the deep, green grass
Dark green grass
Rippling in the breeze at your back.
Parting like a living water, in a growing sea,
At the push of your legs
And resting 'neath the brush of your fingertips.

Run, run til you can no longer run
Run, run

And fall down under a burning golden gaze
In an empty azure face.
Hide breathless in the gentle grasp
Of an earthen bed
And hope you're never found.

Blame

"He said," she said.
"She said he said," he said.
He said, "she said He said."
She said, "He said HE said."

"I said," I said.

2. GROWING UP

Stupidity

The impenetrable darkness filled the room
And the absence of glorious light filled me
With fear
Then before the cold grip of death
Takes my heart
I reason and settle...

I open my eyes.

The First Waltz

One, two, three,
One, two, three,
One, two, three,
Not out loud
In my head
One, two, I'm,
Sorry, No,
Enjoying
Myself? Yes
You dance well
Oops, Sorry,

Are you alright?
Lost it.
Sorry.
Right,

Here we go,
One, two, three,
One, two, three

Walking

The sun is out, it is too warm to hurry.
I'm sitting in this park, on this bench and even the wood is too warm. This one isn't painted.
The sea looks calm, but the small fishing boat might disagree. It looks like a dolphin,
Bouncing in and out of the spray.
The clouds are gathering, but they're still white enough not to panic me.
The light in the park is flicking past as the clouds race silently overhead; it's too warm to race.
I don't really like the noise.
But it isn't noise it's nature and it's quiet. I don't like it.
I put in my earphones and it's time to move. The wind just turned cold.
The sun's still out though.
This song's good, but I can't sing.
Not can't, I can. Proper English; I won't sing.
Not with all these people around anyway.
Sounds of Aerosmith.
The park isn't all that crowded. That's funny. Not funny; strange.
Funny is that stupid dog chasing the birds. It's small. It's white
It's a rat.
A West Highland rat
And his dog.
The owner looks upset. Just let it chase the bloody birds.
Now the birds look upset. And now the lead is out.
This grass slope looks lovely almost beautiful.
"Beautiful weather"
Certainly is. Beats the rain.
"It does at that."
Nice man, don't know him, don't like his dog.
Looks like a big shaved rat.

Bluebells and daffodils and daisies and lions and tigers and bears, o my.
I like that film.
Chris Isaak. Now this is a good song.
Can't do a thing to stop me,
Except stare at me as I sing out loud.
No shouldn't sing
Those houses at the edge of the park look nice. They don't stand out.
I suppose that's the point.
Strange flower.
Painted bench. Broken. Looking closer it's been kicked.
Bastard children. I think its children.
Bastard anyway.
Steps and gravel.
She looks good. I don't think I know her. I won't stare.
She might call the police. "Help,
There's a strange man staring at me." Definitely don't know her
Wish I did. Lovely dog.
Labrador, looks like. Beautiful eyes.
So's the dog.
The whole park looks different from here.
That fountain looks more like the dome of a mosque.
Streets are empty, good
God I'm roasting. If I take this coat off I'll look like a damp lilo.
I think I'll leave it.
Short cut. Strange path, big trees. This shade is
Heaven.
Wonder if it's even close to heaven?
Probably not
Is there a heaven? Does it matter? Not to me.
The sun's out, and it's too warm to hurry.

Painfully So

The saddest truth
of the matter was
She didn't love me
She said, "it's because"
But that was it
My love in a nutshell
No rhyme or reason
No fall into Hell
She said, "it just is"
And I said "well that's fine"
Hope you're happy, hope you're glad
Hope to see you down the line
Down the line
Where my pain can subside
Where yours is much larger
to match your behind.
I want you to see me
So full of the joys
While you have to settle
For men who are boys
Boys who just use you
Like you did to me
Then tell you, "it just is."
And then we will see
How funny it is
To break through a vein
With a knife that won't dull
To twist in my heart
Then enter my skull
And leave no evidence
Of a crime you call love
All with an alibi
That starts with
"It's because."

My Tiny Scar

I have a little scar
It hides on my right hand
The reason that I mention it
Is hard to understand
For though its old and healed
Sometimes it stings as new
Much like the tiny heartbreak stings
Each time I think of you

Pain Without Pain

Short nails cause imprints
In soft fleshy palms
Reminding me
That the thumping pulse in my skull
Is not the only thing
I feel
A tiny tremor
Starting from the ground
An unnatural quake
That feeds the fire breaking out
Behind
My eyes
A face barely visible
Through a strange
Crimson mist
Focuses my attention
While a flaming sword
Of indignant righteousness
Burns in the grip
Of a tightly wound
Fist
Just walk away.

Rainy Sunday

The rain runs in rivulets
Along the crease
That bends the course of your cheek
Between your reddening nose
And the quivering edge of
A downturned pout.

Saltwater drops blend
Seamlessly
With the downpour
That settles like a
Glass masque
Upon your sallow
Pure face.

Your arm hangs loose
At your side
Barely caressing the side
Of your thigh
As the last remaining
Energy from its swing
Subsides.

The darkening of denim
Is all the more apparent
As you turn
And the two tone of
Navy and royal
Blues,
That split your departing silhouette,
Fight for control.

The veil of rain that falls
Closes in over your exit

From the scene
Like the fade out ending
To a melodrama.

Even in this
Biting cold
I feel the warmth of your hand
Where it used to be in mine
And where it ceased to be

The sting of raindrops
Replace the sting on my cheek.

I'm sorry.

Disappointment With Life (In the Afterglow of Lost Teenage Love)

The Sun rose,
Again...

When left behind (Ex Generation)

Moments and mementos.
Memories without memoir.
All sit silent
and ready
to be recalled and recounted in polite conversation
and yet all anybody wants
is one more
single
solitary
second
to bridge a gap
that took a generation to build.

You are not here
and one more bridge is burned
with a vigil flame,
unable to be doused by infinite tears.

Treasure In the Attic

Tattered, torn
and sadly
single eyed.

Weathered and worn
by years,
and years
of pulling and
squeezing and
holding on by a loosely
stitched limb.
But never has love
been given more freely,
with such a fixed
and stoically expressed
face.

"You're not the only cuddly toy,"
Sing monkees on the breeze.
But you were mine
and not mine.

Always someone's,
forever loved.

3. LOVE

SHAUN HARBOUR

My Love is Known

I see the dark, brown dirt
Under the edge of my nails
They offset snowy flecks
And encircle some tails
Of ragged Quick's
and bits of torn skin
That stand like small branches
All Wiry and thin
My 'half moons' are hidden
With dark skin as the cloak

I've a scar on my first joint
From the time it was broken
Smoky grey fingers
Needing cleaned from a day's graft
Crossed with wrinkles and scars
Lead to the simple gold band
And one large freckle that used to be two
Reminds me of how I am
Tied into you
I see time as it wrinkles
And cracks
The hand that holds yours
As we sit in the garden
It only reminds me
That my love can still stand
As comfortable and familiar
As the back of that hand

Bright Lights

Dark night, broken by
Neon Lights, with temptation advertised in
Plain sight of every passing night owl.

Open doors, in the wall of solid light
Begging more customers into the dark
World's core; a world without conscience.

Crawling slow, down familiar streets
No one knows. A world at night where
No one goes, for fear of pain, and hurt, and hate, and recognition.

Painted faces of lost girls paid for
Cheap embraces, from lonely, dark men in
Darker places, where hope of salvation lies dying.

A Pitch black town, who's only saviour
Looks down from behind electricity and neon, shouting
Out loud from below a blue crucifix that

Jesus saves.

Save Me First

I'm drowning
In a desperate tide of sadness

A cold, dense tomb of my own making

Take my hand
And drag me
Lifeless and empty from the dark
And let me breath
In the warm light of your loving smile

The Sound of Silence

Is it
A single hand applauding the imagination
A tipped up tree with no witness
A seashell pressed close when the tide is out.

Is it
The empty corridors of a forgotten school
Hidden in the hiss of a misdialled radio
Found in the space between certainty and doubt.

Is it
The gentle black tears of night over disappearing day
My words at the lonely thought of life
Or my world in the idea of that life without

You.

The Velcro Heart

Heart torn
Rend apart by a difficult conversation
That began with "hello" and ended
Somewhere before "goodbye".
It tore often, with nearly every breath muttered between them,
So often that she felt her life must be
Unnaturally blessed
With the power to heal
The chat was short
Love, not love
Friends, not friends
Friends, not lovers
Must go
Please stay.

The cold light of day shone through
The slowly sealing cracks
And past her open arms
To her last, exposed, raw nerve
Warming her open heart and at last,
Watching him calmly walk away,
She closed the same gaping wounds
As the time before, and the time before that
As secure as she dared
As secure as she could
With a strip of Velcro lies.

Insomnia

Darkened walls rest easy
Against each other for strength
Held tight and bound without seams
By the thick liquid shadows of night's
Black well

Sounds of life whisper from beyond an open window
Whisper of things that dark hearts hide
The soft chill breeze hushes voices
Leaving only the shrill twitter of tiny voices
Laughing in my thoughts.

Eyes closed, no respite
I hold tight for morning's rays
And pray for Morpheus' tender touch
To relieve my world worn thoughts

Death is impossible if you never stop
Life is impossible if you will not stop
Love is impossible if you cannot stop
Stop
The thoughts in my head
And let me wander in the dark.

Let me
Stop.

Heart Shaped Box

Locked and sealed
Cold and hidden
Never to be stolen,
Broken,
Or filled to bursting.

Lost and forgotten
Rusted and unkempt
Never once considered
For the treasure that it holds
Within.

Faded to a memory
Its keeper long since stopped caring
Its upkeep left to chance
This unique, living vessel
Rests
And withers.

And in lonely darkness
Goes
Undiscovered.

A Modern Sonnet

How do I love thee?
Let me count the ways
(Open Spreadsheet Application)
(A1: Z1 highlighted)
(B1=A1+1)
(Drop and drag)
(Z1=Y1+1)
How Do I love thee?
(VALUE!)

Syntax Error?

Time Mends

Bright red apple shine
As I polish my heart with my sleeve
A medal of honour
Ripe for the ripping.
Even broken it remains
Untarnished and easily retrieved
Eventually.

Camels and Straws

Torn stems
Like a woven raft
Over the still,
Clear pool
Which spreads mercurial
And mirror-like
Across the hardwood floor.

Sunlight filters from the warm window
And fractures through the
Weft and warp of the beached
Raft's bow,
Across the room,
And around the hunched, knelt figure,
Picking out
Tiny diamond tears
That glisten
At the foot of the firmly closed door –

Mimicking the slowly
Staining
Tears which drop from
Tightly shut eyes;
Silently rippling on the mirror's surface.

Shredding flower heads
Flutter like rainbow coloured snow
Down the door, reflected in warm waxy varnish
Onto crystal shards

Looking for a vase, which no longer exists.

4. ADULTHOOD

The Voice

There's a voice
No one hears
It talks and allays
My fears
Or sometimes it
Whispers
And spells out the fears
That weren't there
To begin with

Black, oozing, creeping, crushing, hurt-filled
I think just to be hurtful

It breaks
Into song at the drop of a hat.
Then forces the tune
Out of my mouth,
Usually flat,
With little or no
Thought
For pitch or tone.
Or tuning, or that
It has no knowledge of the actual lyrics
And without a care for company
Or any idea of location.

Then it's happy.

I can hear the smile
From it
In its silence,
In my embarrassment
it's happy
And the black melts away.

It laughs loudly
At decidedly dodgy doings
And unintended
Entendre
And inappropriate bovine mooing
It forces me to laugh
Too
Although in fairness
It is usually
Right

I am torn then
Between
the panicked realisation
That I hear voices
That aren't there
And
The panicked realisation
That the voice that isn't really there
Is definitely mine.

Boredom

Blankly staring
at
walls out of focus
while muffled sounds
wash over you
like
neglected waves.
Fluorescent lights
fill the murk
with
harsh white
and
add aches
to a head
already heady
with stress and doubt.

Changing Times for a Paranoid Man

When I was young,
The cat sat on the mat
And the mouse lived in the house
Kids today think in strange ways
And live in a strange world
Where the mouse lives on the mat
And the Cat sits in the car
You can type the way your write
But nobody can write
So what's the point?
Computers talk over the phone
But they can't really talk
And dolls are taking over the world...

Controlling Remotely

The voices from the darkness
Echo in all the corners of the room,
And shout above the crackle
Of the million, tiny torches
That try to fill my eyes.

The lights dance,
Changing colours
And mapping out images of another world.

All able to be removed from my world
With one touch of a single button.

City Square, Friday, 5pm

Flags of all nations clatter and wave bravely in the gusts
as they stand watch over
the busy, bustling
City
Square.

Glints of autumn sunlight
Break across the facades
Giving
Glimpses of beautiful stained glass.
Brought to life
in the dying rays.

An over eager busker,
Over there,
Over the square,
Commits overkill
As he sings Indy pop
Standards
Into a barking speaker
And people try to
Chatter
Over him.

A Skater, determined to be seen,
Comically creates
Giant swings of his
Driving leg and
Steams through the ebbing crowd
Like a locomotive train.

A woman in his path
Breaks step and skips,
Giving him room
To pound by.
Happy,
She tugs her warm coat collar
Tighter
With her free hand
And continues
To tow her handful of balloons
to a waiting seat.
She sits.
Waiting.
She scans her surroundings
For any similarly accessorised sitter
There can be no confusion.

Confused Teens
Smoking their
Oh so grown up fags,
Sit and stand,
staring and splashing,
Like mesmerised toddlers
In the splutter and foam of the
Fountain's
Gurgling waters.

Muffled chatter
from behind
restaurant and cafe windows
from the part filled mouths
Of eternally early eaters
Goes unchanged
And unheard by
Passing pedestrians.

Alone
Outside
At a table for six
She sits.
Her phone barely noticeable
Pressed against her ear
Unlike the Tissue
clenched in fingers.
It covers her broken expression
As she keeps calm
And keeps her open palm
pressed to her covered lips.
But it is too much
And the tissue white flag
Waves
And, head down, she
Weeps.
And tears drop
Onto a notebook
Blurring the
Ink
On the words
"Inoperable" and
"Twins' 6th birthday cake"

Unknowingly
The busker falls silent
And moves on.

A Pram pushing
Mother with no time
Stops at a bench,
puts down her half opened bottle of water,
And lifts baby
For his latest feed

Nearby,
Hidden by rustling
Takeaway wrappings
And squeaky straw dipped
Drinks,
A Young Couple wrestle down
Date night delights.
Her voice is shrill
And full
Of bravado
As her work day spills
From milkshake
Glossed lips.
"I told her"
"I meant it"
"I warned them".
Silent, the listener stays focused
on his sandwich
And wonders
"Is it worth it?"

The early evening rush
Recedes
With the sunlight.
Commuters turn into diners
And stragglers are left
To sit alone
While Elderly gents
fix the world
across a table,
And over coffee,
And under flags of all nations.

Scenes From a Fast Food Restaurant

A bucket of coke
A bucket of fries
Maybe a bucket of chicken wings and thighs
The atmosphere is bright yet bleak
Decked out in fake neo-classic baroque
Slightly spoiled,
Set to mock.

A spill on the floor
A wobbly chair
One customer spits out
An errant hair
You can choose your heart slowing wants
In this semi-clean,
Fast food restaurant

The plastic mouldings on polystyrene
Half columns set into plasterboard walls
Panels of acrylic murals
Show dancing nymphs and
Toga clad maidens
Epoxyed into place
And classically designed cherubim
And seraphim
Cling tightly to banners
Proclaiming
"That traditional MouseKey Sandwich Meal Deal".

The couple sit across a detergent streaked booth table
Young, innocent,
Starry eyed and caught in the moment
Over the best value meal of their lives
The tinkling rattle
Of thin gold bracelets
As the strip lighting glints on the young girl's wrist
Causing a charming, cheeky twinkle
In an already unbearably deep
Ocean blue eye
A reaching hand lifts a fry

Skin touches briefly
An explosion of teen love
A wave of heat brings colour
To the young boy's cheek
And no words can come
So he slurps from his red and white
Striped straw.

Rainy Sunday
Watching cars
Make tracks
Past glass
One view
Cut short
To just a flash
Blowing
Outside
Papers fly
In a dark landscape
And the coffee sits cooling in the cardboard
Next to a slightly disappointing breakfast feast
Of artificial sausage-like meat substance on a rubber egg disc
Accompanied by a powdered excuse for a toasted muffin
A flick of the napkin declares the start of this extravaganza
Look up
World waits
Outside
In the cold.

A cardboard imitation
Of a polystyrene icon
Tumbles through the forced
Colour of a landscaped verge
It scuffs and slides
As a gust drags it
Kicking and screaming across
Black tarmacadam and raised yellow box markings.
It gathers with a group of clones
In a private corner, away from the prying ears
Of four-wheeled customers,
And they rustle their sordid whispers
On how to take over the world.

Life sentence begins with the phrase
Can I take your order here,
Please?
Wasted youth, wasted Saturday,
Wasted
Minimum wage, for minimum gratitude
Maximum expectations for minuscule stars
That let you know I can hand over a bag of food
Without sneezing in it.
I hate you with a passion
Have a nice day
And please
don't give it thought
that your dining pleasure
Is killing me slowly.
Can I take your order here?

Stop, start, stop,
Speak clearly and precisely
Window down,
Plastic clown
Crackling speaker
Getting weaker
Losing the will to live
No extra sauce, no extra fries, no extra drink
No way I'm falling for that
Like a trapped tiger in a safety roll cage chassis
Start, stop, stop, stop, stop.
Sliding glass, sideways and down
Order checked, that's correct, pay the cash
Move along, the franchised conveyer
Next window, order waiting
Bag grabbed, final stretch, move along
Start, stop, engine off
Job done.
Where's my diet coke?

A bucket of coffee
A handful of change
A handful of flavours from their "extended range"
You can choose your heart slowing wants
In this semi-clean, fast food restaurant

The Dark

A film of darkness waves across the heady night
Your warm body cools to the touch
As black and monstrous clouds fill the sky
With a blanket of greys and reds.
The last burning embers of sunlight burn into any space they can
From their perch behind the distant hills
And far away seas.

Throw open the door
Night is here
And with it
A calming touch
A hand on your shoulder
And the dark in your soul

You breathe deeply of the hazy air that surrounds your bed
Lay back and pretend you're alone
Hold your body to a tight line
Until you are sure you are alone
And think of caresses long since past
And dream of kisses still to come
And hope that time can't change a man

Throw back the covers
I am here
And with me
A calming touch
A hand to hold
A dark to match your soul

Touches are slow and painful
Too slow to be real and too painful to be imagined
The thorns complete the femininity of the red rose
As they stab deep into a captured heart
Until it bleeds with the passion
That I can only feel with you
A passion that bends to you with every waking moment.

Throw back your head
You are here
And with us
A passionate embrace
Hands clenched in the moment
And a dark to cover our violent caress.

You Know

You know that moment?

That moment when
Everything around you
Just blurs that tiny bit
Out of focus?
That moment when
Sounds of chat
And laughter
And music
And traffic
And birds
And life
Fall just out of their frequency range
And all that you get
Ringing in your head
Is a dull, droning noise,
Blended with numbing static?

You know that moment
That moment when
The best part of your life seems
A distant memory
Sweet
And innocent

And ever so tantalisingly
Out of reach
And all that remains of your life
Is a broken, busted
Burned out
Routine
That sits on your back
Like a manic child
Weighing down your whole spirit and
Grinding at your temple
With something akin
To a two speed,
Hammer action,
Power drill.

You know that moment?

It's that moment when all it would take is
One single smile from the right person
To stop you seizing,
One single word from the right person
To reconnect you.
One single touch
That proves you are still alive.

Couples Therapy

Sitting, unquestioning,
In silent, resolute
Belligerence
He flicks his finger on the
Small, fiddly, rubber buttons
Of the television remote control
The control that she hasn't touched
In years
Teeth gritted, she listens
To his loud sighing
And constant scratching
Of long dead parts.
Slowly she lifts herself,
Tired bones made heavy
By the weight of a
Long forgotten vow
And her total lack of care.
Backed turned, she hears
His sharp intake of stale air

And the lazy gurgle
Of King-size catarrh
As he makes that last demand
"Brew."
Eyes closed, near to tears, and shoulders low
She shuffles her way
In four year old slippers
Into the small refuge of
Her kitchen.
Staring yet again at
The tarnished
Silver Anniversary
Gift that the kids so kindly
Sent.
She flicks the
Small, fiddly, rubber switch
On the kettle that he hasn't touched.
Teeth gritted,
She lifts a hammer.

Angel
(For an old friend)

A friend of mine went home today
We said goodbye
Tears were shed
And all at once I understood

Destination is constant
Determined at the boarding point
Inescapable
No matter the direction your journeys take

And in the end
All we can ever wish for
Is that someone cares enough
To wave us goodbye.

Grandfather

Tick Tock
Stopped clock.
I know your time has gone.
Your hands remain
Staunchly staid
But time still marches on.
Your face is thinned
Your numbers tinged
With hints of wind and snow
And there you stand
With steady hand
Refusing to let go
Tick tock,
Stopped clock,
You stood so proud and true
I watch the day
Pass into night
And wish you had not
Stopped.

5. PARENTHOOD

Java

Pure black at heart
Only dim earthy light passing
through the fathoms.

A ripple releases
Tiny strands of smoky
Steamy tendrils
Wafting

Into me

Silver cuts like an oar
Splashing drops of dark
Brown wash

Snatched up
and revealing
A watery ring
Proposing we stay together

Forever.

Billy (or How the Boy Was Chosen)

Billy is seven

Billy likes to talk to fairies
Billy has invisible friends
Billy sees the world that remains veiled
Billy knows secrets
About the things that wait in the dark

Billy watches the nymphs on the water
Billy laughs with the imps in the trees
Billy covers his eyes
In a game of hide and go seek
That the tiniest pixie folk invite him to join.

Billy knows the Wee men
Billy knows all the magic tribes
Billy knows beings that are nothing more than a speck of light
And Billy knows that you shouldn't wander in the dark
On narrow paths that break left and right and up and down
In the woods beyond his home.
Billy's parents tell him so.

Billy listens to his parents
Billy tells his parents why he won't wander
Billy lies and tells his parents that he made it up
But Billy tells magic ears that he has to pretend
Or risk never being in the light.

Billy disappears
Billy was here, then Billy was gone
Billy wandered into woods
And onto paths that Billy knows not to wander
Billy thought he knew all the risks of upsetting the wrong colours of magic
Billy left with nothing but a small sack
And Billy left behind nothing but a half-eaten piece of bread and a note.

Billy left the note
Billy wrote his words
Billy wanted people to know
That Billy had to go
And Billy had to go
To the place where the wild things walk in night
And beyond

Billy wanted to be right.

Billy never comes home,
Because wild things in the dark don't always believe in magic either.

Play park

Growling monotone drone
Of a lawn mower
Mimicking the insects that patrol the grass
The nearby school
Playground provides
Screaming and giggling white noise
Covering over the bustling rustling sounds
Of late summer

Young men
In grey uniform tracksuits
Tow status symbols on leads.
Squabbling green ducks
And white swans form a modest battle ground
Upon cool, shimmering,
Sky mirroring waters
Cutting through it all I hear
My true name,
Screamed joyously by the two-year-old girl
Wielding a twig to cast spells on noisy challengers,

"Dad"

She returns triumphant
Huffing and puffing
Laughing and red faced

My pride and joy.

Living

Cry
When the mood takes you
Laugh
Even when it doesn't

Cry hard
Uncontrollably and inconsolably
Without shame
But only for those that matter

Kiss
Every boo boo you believe it will fix
Believe
That every boo boo can be fixed

Never fear the journey
Enjoy it
Never fear the destination
Because everyone goes home in the end

Be good
Be kind
Treat everyone with those four words
in mind

Treat everyone the same
Until they need to be treated differently
And then
Be free
But be justified
In forgetting
Those four words

Let family keep you
grounded
But never let them
weigh you down like an anchor

Create your own thoughts
By being open to others.

Sing and dance
Until you fear your heart may
Stop
And breathe open air
And be happy

Tell great stories
Keep great company
Tell the truth
Keep great secrets

Friends
Will be the truest judge of who you are
Truest friends
Don't judge

Treat faith as your answer
To the most difficult questions
Treat religion as someone else's answer
That you need to question

Love is not a lottery
There are lots of chances to win
But most of them won't
Change your life

And always
And forever
Know I am a word away

And the word is

Daddy.

6. LIFE

Punetry

The irritable doctor lost his patients
With the pointless story
Of a broken pencil.

First Impression

The fat pigeon sits
It sits like a sumo
Atop the gutters of the square
It surveys its feeding ground
Deeply cooing
From within its vast, overfed chest
Two waddling steps
Almost unnoticeable
Beneath its huge ground hugging form

Then
Off into the cool air
Gliding, swooping
Unhurried by the bonds of gravity
Evading the call to Earth
Turning this way and that
Winding its dance
Through the maze of glass and stone
Until at last
It alights in the square
Silently touching down

And a Hitchcockian silhouette
Struts slowly across concrete
Through the moving crowds
To peck at another feed of chips.

Claustrophobe

The stress and strain remained unchanged
Cold, clammy sweat runs icy
And my brow creases
With the cold, dark feeling of misery
It crept upon me and
Now holds my breath hostage
As I fight very urge to scream out loud

Sinew and tendons tighten
As arms hold strong
Between the slowly enclosing walls
And I cannot
Dare not
Will not
Believe that this

Is the end

The air and atmosphere change
And a gentle bell sounds
I move,
Legs of jelly barely supporting,
Me
I turn
As I watch

The others disappear
Behind the closing steel doors.

Sleek

Yellow eyes flicker
In black fur
Half shut moons
With night coiled behind.
Ready for danger
Once this nap is finished.

History is Written by the Victorious

Two great knights
went out to fight
One wild and windy dawn
Said one great knight,
"We'll wait til light,
and fight through the morn!"
T'other knight said, "with my might,
I need no light
to crush you like a pawn!"
"But," said that knight,
"I will delight
in seeing your defeat on the lawn."

From his horse the first knight
called, "The weather's not right,
In this wind my blade can't be drawn."
"Tis true," spoke second knight,
"the day should be bright
and this rain saps even my brawn."
So two great knights
did both alight
and returned homeward with false spun yarns.

Self Awareness

Grace stood on the parapet
and from the bridge to below
She calmly watched the waters swaying
slowly round the
unmoving support.

In attendance - the lights so red and blue
and chants from the massed choir of
Hypocrites and Voyeurs.
Begging her,
Egging her on.

"This one's for you," she thought
and held her hands aloft
Head held high
A beautiful sigh
and the sky
moved before her eyes

And in that moment of madness she concluded
Charity is not at home,
Faith was also gone,
Hope wasn't exactly lost,
but ultimately
there was no saving Grace.

Four

Spring leaves

Exhausted by the July heat of Summer's tirade.
A world of abundant light.
Fields of gold and green.
A hazy patchwork quilt
That heats the earth until
It can take no more
And it throws off its sun beaten blanket
To cool

The Autumn, never seeing Spring,
Sits back and admires
The golden, glowing world
Alive with fire
Dancing in the winds
That flicker and spark
A burning landscape of beautiful
Cold flame

Extinguished
By winter's will,
Leaving behind only bare bones
And skeletons
On which she can build
Her pure, luxurious white, frozen fur
And string it with clear, crystal garlands.
Festive finery for the forgotten beauty.

Spring remembers
And slips off the coat of snow,
Revealing the bouquets
And colours
Of this fresh, new world;
Coaxing dance in the breeze
And love in the green, green grass and
Spring leaves.

Painting Christmas

Crystal flakes drop silently from the heavy sky
A bold grey twisting backdrop against
The swirling patterns turned
In powdery white strokes.

The landscape changes
As the artist's hand
Deftly removes all colour
Taking the fading scenic view
Back to a pure white canvas

Renewed, the season calls for swathes of light
Neon and garish
Strung from trees and lamps
A brand new festive scene
Full of joy and wonderment.

Dreaming of Flamingos (In A Sinatra-esque Fantasy)

I sit encased in darkness
The footlights from the stage catch
The edges of the ice bobbing in a private sea
Of sweet, brown bourbon

Deafened by a sudden fanfare
Blinded in the swinging beams of searching spotlights.

They take to the stage,
A vast wave of golden skin
Sequins
And brilliant smiles.

Hypnotising

They kick, rise, turn, and fall
All in time
Transforming individuals into a single,
Swaying, stepping, twisting, tapping being.

I watch the floating feathers,
Which spare any blushes,
Fanning wings of pink and white.
A pristine procession of wildlife
A flightless display
Of fanciful flesh to titillate and tempt.

Welcome to the jungle.

Escape From a Funfair

The red balloon bobs along
And catches gust after gust
Of warm, summer wind
Taking in the scenery as it passes along.
Fields of shimmering, golden yellow,
Blossoming ranges of orchard trees
Bearing tiny
Shiny replicas
Of this giddy traveller.

It feels the warmth of the late sun
Against its taut skin
And sees tiny silhouettes of
Black birds
Wings outstretched
As if basking on soft, soft sand.

It continues
Unencumbered
By gravity
Superior to the starling
Who soars and brakes and tumbles
Through the ever changing
Turns of the updraughts.

Mazes of dry stone dikes
Cover the sides
Of dragon green hills.
Cutting off the small flocks
Who are nothing but
Meaningless white shapes which litter
Each and every field.

Higher still it climbs
Following the whisper of the cooling air
But allowing no goose-bumps
To surface
Until the only sound left
Is the fluttering rasp of
A nylon ribbon
Twisting and turning as it flows.

The last remnants of the setting sun
Set the opaque bauble alight
Like a glowing star
As the edge of the ocean heaves into view.

And the death of a red balloon
Begins with the crashing of golden, sunset waves.
And a tiny pop.

Christmas Camouflage

Lights brightly,
Even brighter than the stars,
Flicker and twinkle
And flash overhead
From the tinsel-clad, wire lashed
Effigy of a Christmas tree.

It straddles the street
Playing patterns in time
Watched through the eyes
Of a child that never died.

I stand transfixed
And take up space
On a pavement
That needs all the space it can handle
As laden workhorses
Packed with parcels
Run the gauntlet
Through the city
Heading home to the safety
Of the lights on the branches
Of their very own
Plastic tree.

A smile on my lips
A taste of cold winter's air
And I feel warmer than ever
As the snow flutters
Settling in my beard
And turning my cheeks a cosy, rosy
Apple red
Like a giant bauble in a brightly lit
Shop window.

I pull my coat around my stomach
And hide in wide open
Watching the bustle
Of happy, holiday families
And wish for my warmer red coat.

Another year, another day
The time will soon be gone
But the child inside will remember forever
While I wait
For next year
And a chance to briefly mingle
Again.

Let It All Wash Away

White, blue, silver, blue
The traffic flows with every conceivable hue.
Past our silence.
Silver, black, red, blue, red
I count cars with white knuckles pressed,
Sealing my mouth from begging and my eyes from weeping.
Silver, silver, green, blue
A metallic wave, blurred by my half closed, tearful, praying, eyes,
Crashes ever onward
Into the shortening light.
Grey, green, grey, black
The glass between us muffles sound
Into that of a seashell's ocean.
Black, black, black, black
The end of the world drops away with the tide
And a final glimpse of you;
Caught in the undertow.
I can't bring myself to swim along with the tide
So I sit
And do nothing
Except slip off a black tie.

ABOUT THE AUTHOR

Shaun Harbour is a Scottish author and poet who published his first children's book in 2014. Written for his daughter "The Robin and The Wish" garnered rave reviews and led to the writing of this collection of poetry.
He is 40 years old and lives in Perthshire with his family.

Printed in Great Britain
by Amazon

42206850R00056